GW00499587

REALISE YOUR

DIAMOND SELF

A Journey
back to Wholeness

Author's Comment

It is my heartfelt desire you experience all that you intended in this lifetime. You may not get what you think you want, likewise you receive what you need. As you surrender to your Higher Self, the wisest part of you, your bliss far outweighs any challenges, for a more joyful and fulfilling life.

A key to unlocking this Lighter way of Being is through taking responsibility for your life, to know it is you in the driving seat. Humanity's biggest self-imposed obstacle is resistance to change. Through recognising that change has a purpose for your highest good, it is easier to transition. This book invites you to Apply and Integrate *The Six Pillars* and *18 Facets* into your daily life. Through Embodying this new way of Being, you become the powerful co-Creator that you are.

You are never alone. Your Higher Self is guiding you and there are Earth Angels and Light Beings around you. Realise your Diamond Self is a reminder you can do anything you set your Heart and Mind to do.

Realise your Diamond Self ~ A Journey back to Wholeness
Copyright to Jane Red Path @ 2021 All Rights Reserved
First Publication in 2018. No part of this Publication to be reproduced
without the consent of the Author - ISBN: 9798764603254

Author Jane Red Path
www.walktheredpath.com
Foreword by Michiel Kroon
www.michielkroon.com
Testimonial Dr Lorna A. Collins
www.lornacollins.co.uk
Proofread by Molly Websdell

May you Realise
all that you are
and Experience all
that you Intended

The Six Pillars

and *18 Facets*

An Alchemy Toolkit
to Realise your Diamond Self

You are an unfolding Masterpiece
As you Journey with
The Six Pillars and *18 Facets*
they gently and beautifully
shine their Light
onto any unseen layers
of who you are not
to reveal the Gift and Magnificence
of who you are

Content

Content

YOUR JOURNEY

Content

Content

...

Foreword by Michiel Kroon

How can we raise the collective vibration amidst belief systems that pit people against each other? Fear based thinking separates communities and gets amplified by their engagement in battles between the dark and the light. In recent years, many friendships have been lost because of failing to see that we *are* light, and we all come from the same Source.

I believe that bringing people together in harmony raises the vibration. We need to step away from indifference, or partial indifference to those with a different belief system. We need to remember that we are all one tribe, and lend our light to those who feel stuck.

We all know this deep down. But in the face of crisis, many retreat into a circle in which their beliefs are confirmed. The circle is their community, both on-line and in person. In many circles, a fear of anything and anyone outside of that circle has started to develop. Some even go as far as saying there is almost no use in talking to anyone outside of their circle.

One question I love to ask is, what would Divine Creator do? Through the eyes of the Cosmic Heart Source, everyone is a perfect aspect of the Divine, and worthy of Divine Guidance. The Divine has no judgment and does not need to save anyone, but never gives up on anyone either.

Foreword by Michiel Kroon

The Six Pillars help you to step into the Divine Light, so that you start to communicate Light. And *the 18 Facets* assist in clearing the Old Paradigm from your system. As a result, you are elevated to a whole new vibration in which you are beyond any resonance with dysfunctional patterns in the collective.

One of the best reminders of Truth is to point out your power as Creator. And each page of this book does exactly that. The words are reminders that literally nothing on the outside has the power to affect your Divine Light.

By taking in these reminders, and taking pauses to deeply receive them, you start to awaken to the Truth of who you really are. This is the Truth that is not contaminated with fear-based beliefs, and therefore does not polarize or separate. You realise that you are a facet of Divine Creator, and that you are here to shine your Heart Light into the world.

Each time you remember this, you create a space for more Love. In this space, old patterns and energies likely come to the surface. This is the integration process, in which you are invited to keep your eyes on the light. If you go into distraction, the Universe will remind you, through its many messengers, of your True Self and your Path of Light. Some of these messengers are Angels, Ascended Beings, Cosmic Guides and Elementals. They are all around you to embrace you and to give you guidance on the path.

Foreword by Michiel Kroon

More and more, you come back to the Heart, which is your portal back to the Source. And through this process, you are contributing to the collective ascension, without absorbing any of the old energies. You are simply raising the vibration by following the Joy in your Heart.

In this knowing of your True Self, you then naturally start to remind others of their power too. This ignites Heart to Heart conversations, which also get expressed as speeches, poems, songs, dances, and artworks. In other words, the expression of Unconditional Love, in which fear and darkness are exposed as illusions.

As I set the Intention to
become all that I AM,
I let go of expectation
and need to measure my worth
Through simply allowing
a glorious unfolding
my Becoming
is immeasurable

YOUR COMPANION GUIDE

In the face of adversity
I lower my Awareness from the head
into the welcoming Heart
to allow for a new way of Being to emerge
With gentle Encouragement
from the Neutral Mind
it enables a resting place, a safe haven
for the Pure Potentiality of the Heart
and the resonance to receive the Gift

You are an
unfolding Masterpiece

The Six Pillars are Fractals of Light
reflecting the Light within you
but have simply forgotten
As you Invoke the Pillars,
you call in the Qualities
of your Higher Self,
the part of you that is in continual
Harmony with itself

The Pillars act as a Reminder
shining their Light onto *18 Facets*,
18 characteristics of human behaviour,
that you are being invited
to Master at this time
They become more than words on a page
more of a Resonance of your Being

.

Each Pillar and Facet
seamlessly flow into the next
as you build and develop
the most important relationship
the relationship you have
with yourself

Reconnect to
the Alchemist Within

Alchemy takes place when you
replace an uncomfortable thought
with a heartfelt response
Each time you choose
to respond from the Heart
you are Activated to feel more alive
because you Remember
who you are

It is when you take Responsibility
for yourself and your life
to Embody the Qualities you seek that
you allow for Transformational Change

The Six Pillars take you on a Poetic Journey
to let go of the chatter of the mind
and reconnect to the peacefulness of the Heart

As you Invoke the Pillars
their Light infuses your Aqueous Body
the Water transmutes into its Crystalline Form
and your base nature transforms
into its Diamond Essence

Remember your
Magnificence

As you reconnect with
the Frequency of your Heart
you Reclaim the lost parts
to come back to the Wholeness that you are

The Portal is through Mastery of the Mind
a quietening that enables you
to reconnect with your Heart
the part of you that holds
your highest intelligence
As you deepen your Awareness
of each Pillar and Facet
you deepen the Relationship with yourself
to reveal long-buried treasures
simply through the Gift of Being
who you are

The more you choose
to incorporate these values
into each moment of your day
You peel back unseen layers of who you are not
to reveal the Gift and Magnificence
of who you are

A Reminder of
Life's Simplicity

The Six Pillars remind you
what the Heart already knows
It is the mind that likes to complicate
Words initially outside of you strike a deep cord,
a Remembrance that resonates
at the core of your Being
bringing you back to your natural state

Birthed from a place of Profound Presence
The Six Pillars take you on a Journey
to reconnect with your Innate Stillness
a place that is continually
residing within

The words hold a Frequency
to create a Lighter template within you,
to move beyond the limitations of the mind
into the welcoming and expansive Heart

Similar to the moment
between the Inhale and Exhale,
the spacing between words and paragraphs allow for
pauses of Reflection, Integration and Recalibration
to enable a deeper connection to your Heart

Life is your Learning Ground
and your Playground

Through Invoking the Pillars
you draw into your life
the people and situations you need
to Grow and Glow
Life gives you Choice Points
where self-limiting patterns of behaviour
play out in your life

When you choose to respond
from your Heart, versus the head,
an internal chemistry takes place
to allow for a new way of Being
to come to you
and through you

The more you incorporate
these Six Values into your life,
to Embody their Qualities
there is less of a need to look outside yourself,
because you know you have everything within
The ultimate aim is to
Embody each Pillar and Facet
into each moment of your life
to Be the change you seek

Activate your
Diamond Light Body

Journeying with *The Six Pillars*
enable you to access
your Highest Frequency
for a lighter experience
Each Pillar is an aspect
of your Heart frequency,
expressed through words
As you move deeper into matter
each Pillar offers an Affirmation,
a Frequency that enables the mind
to better access the qualities of the Heart

Each Pillar holds
3 Facets of your Diamond Self
Three expressions of a Pillar's Quality
illuminating the Light and Shadow within you
and how you choose to interact
with this aspect in your life

When you choose
to respond from the Heart
your Heart Flame is Activated
to Align with your Diamond Light Body
and the Diamond Light Matrix
a Gateway to your Multi-Dimensional Self

Incorporate *The Six Pillars*
into your Daily Life

Intention

Through setting the Intention
to Incorporate *The Six Pillars*
into your life,
the Universe conspires
to make it happen

There is no right or wrong way,
your Heart knows

Likewise, encourage habits
which reconnect
with your Heart

Sit Quietly
Lower your Awareness
from the head into the Heart
Rest there
a few moments

Notice the Breath,
without changing it,
simply Observe

Incorporate *The Six Pillars*
into your Daily Life

Invocation

Go to the Pillar or Facet
to which you Feel
most drawn

Read the Pillar or Facet silently
or speak it out loud
with feeling

As you read the words of a Pillar or Facet
bring your focus up to the Third Eye
the point between the brows.
Breathe,
gently hold your Awareness there

Bring your Feeling Awareness
into the Heart
Breathe into the Consciousness
behind the Words
Infuse and Permeate
their energy into your Being

Incorporate *The Six Pillars*
into your Daily Life

Application

Cultivate the ability to become
the Observer of your life,
to notice what is happening
within and around you

Ask for Guidance
Your Higher Self is ready
to assist you at all times

Why has this situation come into my life?
What is the Wisdom I AM being Gifted?
What Loving Action can I take
for my Highest Good?

Listen with the Heart
Be patient with yourself
Journal your Experience
Feel Gratitude. Always.

You are
the Diamond

When you Realise
you are the Diamond and
you are the Pillars
You have come back
to yourself

Notice any resistance
to Journey with the Pillars,
a Pillar or Facet may evoke
uncomfortable thoughts or feelings
Love that part of you,
it simply wishes to be felt and held

Your seeming obstacles
are your greatest Gifts.
You have chosen to Experience,
Transmute and Transform what
no longer serves you into what does.
When a seeming challenge
shows up in your life
Thank it,
for it is your Teacher.

YOUR JOURNEY

There is a Crucible of Fire
that takes place
when a deeply uncomfortable pattern
is felt by the Journeyer,
where such an intensity and pressure
are felt,
that the water in the body is Crystallized
and the carbon has no choice
other than to become the Diamond

The First Pillar

I HAVE THE FREEDOM

TO CHOOSE

My life is an ever
unfolding Masterpiece
Through choosing
what and how I Experience
Life empowers me to Realise
I can do Anything
I set my Heart and Mind to do

The Facet of
ACCEPTANCE

As I let go
of the need to control
I surrender to this moment
and reconnect to
the innate stillness
within

As I savour this moment
the point at which
I gently lay my focus
I invite a softening
a resting place
for the Pure Potentiality
to arise within

Through acknowledging
the Gift in every situation
I hold the resonance
to receive the Gift

The Facet of
OWNERSHIP

When adversity knocks at my door
it is a gentle nudge
to make a change
Any feelings of frustration
or disappointment
offer valuable feedback
in the unfolding of who I AM

As I take full responsibility
for the choices I have made
I realise I AM a Co-Creator
with all of life
Through choosing to Act versus React
I invite an unfolding awareness
and the Guidance I need
to create positive change

There are no mistakes
Within the Spirals of Consciousness
life offers new levels of awareness
waiting to greet me
whenever I AM ready

The Facet of
EMPOWERMENT

As I AM a co-Creator
with all of life
I attract everything
that comes into my experience
My choices of today
reflect the outcomes
of my tomorrows

As I choose each Thought, Word,
Action and Behaviour
I create my evolving reality
Through expecting the Highest Outcome
in every situation
I bring my Self back into alignment
with all that I AM

My inner world
becomes my outer world
My outer world reflects back
my inner world

The Second Pillar

I VALUE
WHO I AM

As I choose to Value
and Nurture my Self
I reconnect to the Innate Stillness within
As I Listen to and Act
on my Inner Guidance
I come into alignment with
my True Essence
and all that I AM

❖

The Facet of
SELF-LOVE

As I Invest in my Self
I cultivate my True Nature
The more I feel my Natural State
The more I know who I AM

As I commit to valuing my Self
I affirm that I value
who I AM
As all life is a Reflection
The world comes to value me too

As I honour my Self
I align with my Highest Good
As I align with
my Highest Good
I align with the Highest Good
of all those around me

The Facet of
COMPASSION

Through Discipline,
Reverence and Devotion
I set my Self free
Likewise my resistance does not define me
It is simply an invitation
to Love my Self
more

As I AM compassionate with my Self
at all times
I respond with Loving Action
Even if that means
simply Being

Through being kind to my Self
I allow a softening, a grace,
Mercy from something Far Greater
I shift from me to we

The Facet of
CONNECTION

Self-Love and Self-Care,
in the form of
time alone,
bring me back to my centre
The more I access
this calm Inner State
I AM no longer lost
in the midst of expectation

Through honouring my Self
and my needs
I establish a clear sense
of who I AM
I know where I start
and the other finishes

I AM here to know my Self
Likewise, I AM are here to know my Self
through others

The Third Pillar

I CHOOSE
GRATITUDE

The Pendulum of Life may swing
one way and then the other
As I become the Observer of
the fluctuations of the mind
to experience Non-Attachment,
Acceptance and Gratitude
I AM able to live from the
Infinite Joy in my Heart

The Facet of
BEING

As I develop
a sense of Being
I cultivate a deeper awareness
beyond my sense of Self
Through being fully present
to the moment
I reconnect to something
Far Greater
than my physical eyes can see

As I pause between activities
I Assimilate, Integrate and Recalibrate
Within this space of allowing
life is able to choose me
instead of me chasing life

Simply Being
maintains and sustains my Balance
It is vital to Realising
my goals

The Facet of
RECEIVING

Through Giving, I create the space
within me to receive
As I Receive, I gift others
the joy of giving
each perpetuating the infinite cycle
of abundance within and around me

Through knowing
I AM worthy to receive
I match a Frequency
to receive the Gift
Through practicing the Art of Receiving
I affirm I AM ready
to receive the Gift

As I receive freely
I practice Self-Love and Self-Worth
As I give freely
I affirm that I AM abundant
and live in an abundant world

The Facet of
FLOW

As I allow life to unfold
in whichever way
it wishes to go
The River of Life carries me
As I reconnect to this endless stream
a seamless path appears
One that is calling me Home

Through the practice of non-Attachment
to all things
I reconnect to my centre
From this point of Neutrality
all life is able to come to me
and through me

As I align with
the Universal Flow
I tap into all of Creation
and the Creation of all things

The Fourth Pillar

I TRUST LIFE AND
LIFE TRUSTS ME

As I trust deeply and completely,
life flows through me
As I reconnect with
the Unconditional Love in my Heart
I feel the Peacefulness and Expansiveness
that sits at the core of my Being
In choosing to live in the knowledge
that I AM Safe and Loved
the Universal Abundance comes to meet me

The Facet of
SELF-BELIEF

As I reconnect to the
Joy in my Heart
I no longer look
outside of me
As I value my Self
from the inside out

As I practice Self-Reliance
I affirm that I value
who I AM
When I find and maintain my centre
I reconnect to the all-Knowing
and all-Seeing part of me

Through affirming who I AM
I value my Self
And in turn, others come
to value me too

The Facet of
SYNCHRONICITY

As I let go of attachment to
how and when life unfolds
I reconnect to Divine Timing
As I Co-Operate with life
a synergy presents itself
that goes beyond time and space

As I cultivate being fully present
to the moment
I AM able to let go of any sense of urgency
I may not yet know
how the jigsaw fits together
but come to realise that everything
is unfolding as it should

Although I may feel tested at times
I know there is a better outcome
waiting to unfold
One that I can't yet see
My Higher Self that sits
at the top of my Tree of Life
is able to see the big picture
and will draw those experiences I need

The Facet of
PARTICIPATION

As I participate in life
I enjoy the opportunities
that life brings
Through celebrating
my Unique Expression,
in the knowledge that each of us
is one part of the whole,
I reconnect to the Source
from which I came

As I AM confident in
sharing who I AM
and what I feel to share
I AM choosing to participate
In doing so, I discover previously
unknown and unseen parts of me
that help me Remember who I AM

I AM grateful for everyone in my life
as they show me how to become
the best version of who I AM

The Fifth Pillar

I EXPRESS ALL OF ME
TO BECOME
ALL THAT I AM

In being True to my Self
I create a Clear Channel
and Fertile Ground
to receive the Inspiration,
Guidance and Abundance
that is waiting to come through me
As I choose to live from my Truth
and Authenticity, there is no effort
as I AM simply being who I AM

The Facet of
SELF-EXPRESSION

As I express the Diversity
of who I AM
I feel gratitude for
the Depth and Breadth of my Being
Life, in turn, lifts its veil
to reflect back a whole new world

As I step into the Fullest Expression
of who I AM
I let others see what I would prefer to hide
As I reveal
what I AM most afraid to show
I realise these are the parts most want to see
It is equally
my Vulnerability and my Strength
that reunites and binds us together

The more I express my Unique Personality
the more of who I AM comes through
In this Freedom of Expression
my heart opens
and I invite others to do the same

The Facet of
AUTHENTICITY

Through living in my Truth
I create a transparent world
Through letting go
of what no longer serves
I create the space to let in
all that does

An honest life
is a courageous life
As I let go of the need for approval
I create a Clear Channel
for new Experiences,
Opportunities and Synchronicities
reflecting back
who I have become

The relationship I have with my Self
sets the tone for all my relationships
When I live with integrity
I know who I AM
and others know me too

The Facet of
RECLAMATION

As I reclaim
my lost parts
I come back into the Fullest Expression
of who I AM
As I let go of a lesser version
I reconnect to the expansiveness
that sits at the core of my Being

Through Loving my Self
deeply and completely
I create a safe place to reclaim
what was once lost
and has now returned
As I let go of the unforgiveness
and separation in my Heart
I reconnect to the Oneness of all things

Only when I have experienced
my fragmented Self
can I know the whole
Only when I know who and what I AM not
can I experience all that I AM

The Sixth Pillar

AS I LIVE FROM
THE JOY IN MY HEART
I MERGE WITH
THE DANCE OF LIFE

As I choose to live from the
Fullest Expression of who I AM
I reconnect with the Expansiveness
and Potentiality of all that is
Free to be all of me,
I feel Loved, Loving,
Grateful and Alive

The Facet of
EMBODIMENT

Life is a mirror
Each relationship offering
an outer reflection
of my inner world
Guiding me back to the
best version of who I AM

I AM grateful for
all the relationships in my life
as I know they are here
to support me
Each person reflecting back
an aspect of who I AM
I let go of judgment, for it is why I AM here
The Path of Unconditional Love

Through Embodying the Qualities
I revere in others
I raise my Vibration
to Recognise
the other person is me

The Facet of
TRANSMUTATION

It is easy to Love those
I deem as loveable
At some level, I also choose to attract
people and situations that test my ability to Love
As I choose Love over adversity
each time
my Heart expands into a Greater and Deeper
experience of Love and Joy

As I choose to see the Higher Purpose
in a seemingly challenging relationship
I feel Gratitude for the
opportunity given to me
As I choose to act from
a place of Unconditional Love
I AM elevated to the Highest and
best version of who I AM

Through Application and Integration
of this new way of Being
I reconnect to the Alchemist Within

The Facet of
FREEDOM

As I let go of the self-imposed limitations
I release the shackles that keep me stuck
in the lower mind
As I reconnect to my Joy and Inspiration
I merge with the Universal Intelligence
that sits at my Heart

As I lower my focus
into the Dominion of the Heart
I experience Gratitude for all things
Free to be all of me
I expand into an ever greater
experience of Love

As this renewed Freedom emanates
from the whole of my Being
I realise it was me all along
For I chose this Journey
to experience who and what I AM not
The carbon and water have Crystallized
to become
the Living Diamond that I AM

Awakening to
your Unique Gifts

The Six Pillars and *18 Facets*
Awaken
your Divine Spark
to welcome in
the Resonance of your Divinity

This Resonance
holds
the Frequency of
your Unique Expression

Through integrating
your True and Higher Self
your Heart opens
to Realise the Love
that you are
and to Express this Love
through your
Creative Expression

Sharing your
Unique Gifts

Follow your
Heart

Do what you Love and
Love what you Do

Focus on
your Strengths

Lightly hold the Highest Vision
of yourself and your life

Take Loving Action

Play. Be Curious.

Own your Sovereignty

Be You. Always.

About the Author

Jane Red Path is a Writer,
Yoga and Mindfulness Teacher.

Through her self-limiting beliefs and patterns,
she discovered Yoga to welcome
long-forgotten Peace of Body and Mind.

The Six Pillars were born following a
call to the Sacred Mount Shasta,
culminating over a 4-year period
into what you see today.

Given the Yogic name Jeetprem Kaur
meaning Love through Adversity,
an aspect of her calling is to
Empower others to see the Gift in all of life

Jane is passionate to inspire others
to Realise their Unique Gifts and
joyously participate in creating
a harmonious Earth-World.

Acknowledgements

Our Friends, Family, Animals
and Environment create the
perfect setting for us to
Learn, Grow and Glow.

I thank my Mum Gill, Dad John,
sister Vickie and brother-in-law Phil,
step-Dad Mike, step-Mother Janet,
nephews Callum and Sam,
Grandparents Joe, Edith,
Bill and Hilda.

I thank my Spirit Guides:
my Guardian Angel,
the Lemurians,
the Ascended Masters,
my Animal Guides,
Mother Earth and the Elementals.

Printed in Poland
by Amazon Fulfillment
Poland Sp. z o.o., Wrocław
22 August 2023

bc6cba29-c8f7-467f-af59-1b03544e6ddfR01